Vision Boards Made Easy

A Step-by-Step Guide for All Ages

Tania Chumbley

BALBOA.
PRESS
A DIVISION OF HAY HOUSE

Contents

Acknowledgements ix
Introduction xiii

Chapter 1: What Is a Vision Board? 1
Chapter 2: What You Need to Get Started 7
Chapter 3: Vision Boards for Adults 9
Chapter 4: Vision Boards for Children 31
Chapter 5: Vision Boards for Teenagers 47
Chapter 6: Phrases to Use or Not Use on Your Vision Board 61
Chapter 7: Attracting What You Want: Six-Month, One-Year,
          and Five-Year Plan 65
Chapter 8: Programming Your Day 71
Chapter 9: Making a Vision Board Using Your Computer 73

About the Author 75
About the Book 77

**The biggest adventure you can ever take
is to live the life of your dreams.
Oprah Winfrey**

Acknowledgements

Thank you to my wonderful husband, Mark, who has always supported me in all my many varied interests. I also thank my beautiful children, Amber and Jake, for being proud of me as I write and publish this book. To my mum, Maria, my dad Michael and my sister Karen: You always let me be the free spirit that I am and always saw the potential in me. Thanks to my friends June, Annie, Penelope, and Kellie: You all believed in me. And look, I did it!

I would also like to thank Oprah Winfrey. You inspired me to be the best that I can be. I am the person I am today because of all your aha moments and many teachings from the time you started in the nineteen eighties through to now.

To Louise Hay. Thank you from the bottom of my heart for your many books, CD's, and videos. Your positive affirmations have helped so many thousands of people transform their lives for the better. You are brilliant and truly one of the best teachers of our time.

Make your vision board.

Look with positive feelings.

Surrender—let it go.

Believe it will happen!

Tania Chumbley

Introduction

I was born in the nineteen seventies, and from the time I was ten years old, I noticed I was different from others. It wasn't till I hit high school that I noticed that I had psychic abilities. I was very much judged in my teens as being too sensitive. Authority figures made comments such as, "You don't do that, do you?" Because of this, I shut off my abilities and did not use them again until my father was diagnosed with chronic myeloid leukaemia. I thought that he was on borrowed time, and I decided to open myself up again. I needed support and guidance to get through that emotional time. My psychic abilities blossomed again, and my father also had a perfect bone marrow match from his sister. This, in turn, helped him go into remission. I have kept using my abilities ever since and feel that I can't be 100 per cent myself if I don't.

In 2005 the bestselling book *The Secret* came out. Many thousands of people were in love with its message, and a DVD was soon released too. Rhonda Byrne, the author, appeared on the *Oprah Winfrey Show* broadcast worldwide as a must-see television event. I watched the episode and read the section on vision boards, and I was inspired to make one myself. I immediately did just that, and I was overwhelmed at how I manifested what I wanted and saw the results within one or two years, and some things I put on my vision boards came at a really fast rate.

In early October 2010, I heard on the nightly news that Oprah would be coming to Australia the following December and that she was giving away three thousand tickets to see her live in Sydney. A friend of mine rang and asked me if I was entering, as she knew what a huge fan I was of Oprah, so I went online and entered. I rang my mum to ask her if she would like to come with me if I won tickets. My mum said, "Of course, yes." After getting off the phone with her, I immediately made a new vision board. I found pictures of Oprah in a magazine and the words, "Win tickets to see Oprah." I cut them out straight away. Once I finished making my board, I looked at it every now and then when I felt good. I stuck it on the wall in my bedroom. On 7th November at teatime, while watching the nightly news, I heard that the lucky winners had been notified by email. My phone rang, and it was my mum asking if I knew whether I had won. I said that I hadn't had a chance to check yet. I got off the phone with her, and then I went and checked my email. There in front of me was a message from Harpo Productions, stating that I had won two tickets to Oprah's morning show in Sydney on 14 December. I jumped up and down and screamed with my kids for at least fifteen minutes. The neighbours must have thought that I was in trouble. I rang my husband, and then I rang my mum and told her to sit down. When I gave her the great news, she screamed as well. It was an amazing experience to win the tickets, my husband was shocked. He said that there could be something to this vision board stuff, as so many wonderful situations were coming true.

After the adults in my classes had success making vision boards, I had the idea that it was time to work with children and teenagers. It was like a guardian angel whispered this in my ear. I have worked in a school since 2007, and when I had my first chance to do vision boards with children, I called them treasure maps. I also worked with a large group of children in a care facility outside of school hours. They all found it easy and enjoyed the session immensely. I noticed that the older children had no problems in doing this activity, and this gave me the insight that this could cover reception-aged children right through to adults.

I led positive development classes at home with a group of women, and I decided to do a lesson on Vision boards. It was very successful; they loved making the boards and found the activity relaxing and easy. Most of the women had situations and objects come to them in a short period of time as a result.

I feel that more people in the world need to know about this secret, and if each person made one or two vision boards a year, they would notice positive changes in a short amount of time. Vision boards help you make your mind up as to what you would like to help manifest in your life. The universe can only bring you what you desire once you know what that is. This book is an easy, step-by-step guide. It can be used as a workbook, so you can cut out the affirmations inside and paste them to paper. *Vision Boards Made Easy* is great to use for all age groups, from kindergarten-aged children right up to adults.

The sky's the limit with what you can bring into your life using vision boards. I have manifested better health, increased confidence, my first new car (after many second-hand ones), material things, home decor, holidays, lovely friends, and better family relationships, just for starters.

May this book, which means the world to me, make your dreams come true and help manifest desires for you, your friends, and your family. It would also make a great gift for someone special.

And may the universe deliver many beautiful gifts. You deserve them.

Tania Chumbley

What Is a Vision Board?

A vision board is a visual imagery tool used to attract to you what you want.

How Does It Work?

A vision board works once you have decided what it is that you want. This is a major problem for most people, as it's hard to make a decision. That's why they don't have what they want. Once you have made a decision, the universe can manifest your goals and desires. It's not magic. It's the law of attraction. We all have vibrational energy around us that works when we are feeling good. It flows out into the universe with the intention of bringing our goal or desire.

Stay Positive!

When making your board, it's extremely important to be positive and happy. You create wonderful things on your vision board when you are in a good mood.

Your Vision Board Is About You!

Your vision board is all about your goals and dreams, so the focus is on what you want, not on what others may want. It's a wonderful exercise for focusing on your needs and putting yourself first. We don't have power over other people; we only have control over our own lives. A friend of mine once said, "Can you make a vision board for me?" I told her it wouldn't work because she didn't make

1

it herself—she didn't put her energy and intention into it. Therefore, if a friend wants to attract something, he or she will need to do a vision board.

Play Happy Music in the Background

Hearing happy music raises your vibrational frequency, which makes you feel fabulous; this allows creativity to flow through you. Inspirational music therefore allows emotion to flow through the body, which in turn gives you insights and great ideas to help manifest your desires.

Then You Must Surrender It!

Once you've looked at the images, words, and so forth on your board with good feelings, you must surrender them. Believe that the thing or things will come to you, and then let it go. Look at your board occasionally when you're happy, and trust that all will go well. Put your positive energy into it; that's how simple it is!

Your Thoughts, Feelings, and Words Are Powerful

We have over sixty thousand thoughts a day. Isn't that mind boggling? So, it's crucial that your thoughts are positive most of the time. Your vibrational frequency of good feeling, as I call it, needs to be in a happy neutral mode to prevent being at a negative frequency.

Make sure that you stay positive as much as you can. When you are, you think positive thoughts, you feel fabulous, life is good, and your body feels light. Through their magnetism, positive people are attractive to others. They are less prone to illness and love being around people. They also have a great outlook on life.

When you think negative thoughts, you get a horrible uncomfortable feeling in your stomach, and you say negative words. These make you more prone to suffer from low self-esteem. Your body posture is usually slumped; you may also avoid eye contact and prefer your own company most of the time. Being in a negative frame of mind for extended periods of time may lead to depression and a weak immune system.

The thoughts in our minds are just as strong as the ones we say out loud. The energy of our thoughts comes out through our auras and brings similar things and situations into our lives. This puts a perspective on how amazingly powerful we are and reinforces that anything is possible.

To turn your intentions into reality, all that is needed is to be positive, be in a good mood, and use phrases such as "I am," "I can," "I now …" and so forth when you speak or make a decision.

For example, you might make the following statements: I am doing great. I can do anything once I set my mind to it. I now have great health in my life.

We don't need to see electricity to know it exists. We know it does, as we use it all the time. Similarly, our thoughts have energy behind them that gets pushed out into the universe to attract what we are thinking about. So, we need to be aware of our thinking. When we have a negative word or sentence, it's helpful to change it to a positive one.

So, what's stopping you? I'm excited for you, as now you know how creating vision boards can really work for you. Let's get started.

Negative Thoughts brings back to you negative feelings and situations.

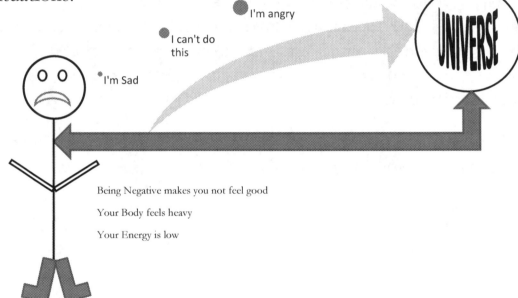

I'm angry

I can't do this

I'm Sad

UNIVERSE

Being Negative makes you not feel good

Your Body feels heavy

Your Energy is low

Being negative can create low self-esteem and confidence.

Positive Thoughts brings back to you positive feelings and situations.

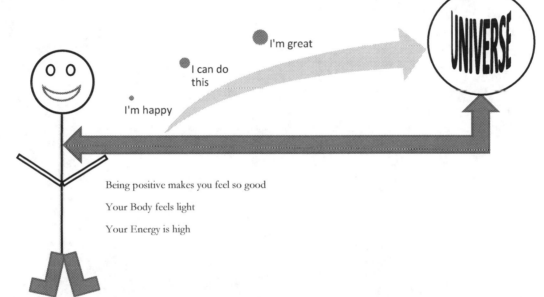

I'm great

I can do this

I'm happy

UNIVERSE

Being positive makes you feel so good

Your Body feels light

Your Energy is high

Being positive can create high self-esteem and confidence.

5

What You Need to Get Started

Poster paper or cardboard, any size

Magazines, newspapers, or photos

Food brochures

Scrapbooking stick-on pieces

Stickers or tape

Scissors (straight edge and with patterned edges), glitter, or ribbons

Markers, crayons, coloured pencils, charcoal, lead pencils, pens, or paint

Glue and pencil sharpener

Ruler, stencils, tracing paper

Cork board and thumb tacks

7

Instructions

Think about what you really want to happen for the next twelve months.

It's great to make a vision board at the start of a new year, but you can do one at any time.

Make sure that it is about your goals, not someone else's goals, as you cannot affect another person's destiny.

Make sure that you have a large desk or a big clear space on the floor where you can spread out all your magazines and sheets of paper.

Go through your magazines, newspapers, photos, and the like, and look at pictures and words that inspire you, related to the subjects you've chosen.

Use the phrase, "I am ..." at the start of a sentence on the board. For example, writing and saying, "I am happy," will start manifesting the emotion, and more happiness will come to you in this way.

Cut out the letters, words, pictures, photos, and so on that you love and place them on your cardboard or paper. Move them around until you are happy with where they are. You can also draw sketches or add wording by hand with Markers or pens.

Listed on the following pages are words that you can cut out and use for your vision board and topics to focus on. I have included positive affirmations as well, or you can write up your own. I have separated the chapters for adults, children, and teenagers to make it easier for each age group to use.

Once happy with the placement, you can start to glue everything down. It doesn't matter if the pictures overlap.

As the things represented by your vision pictures and sentences materialize, you can cover them with new pictures to use the same vision board. That way, you only have one vision board at a time.

Vision Boards for Adults

Why Vision Boards Are Great for Adults

Adults using vision boards can make some amazing goals and situations happen. Because of the person's focus and intention, the universe moves things and situations to create the positive outcome.

The most popular vision boards for adults contain a label in each corner of the page for a particular topic—for example, travel, love, work, and health. As described previously, adults cut out pictures and write sentences of the relevant subjects. You can focus on a few areas at the same time.

You might like to use some of the affirmations that I included on the next few pages.

Over the years that I have made vision boards and worked with others to show them how to do it, one thing is certain. Each person, including myself, has manifested something or many things from what they put on their vision board.

Your board can be used for so many areas of your life, and it's not hard to put together. All it takes is some paper, scissors, glue, and writing tools.

You can do a vision board by yourself or with friends or family. Children can participate as well.

Give it a go, and see what happens!

9

Vision Board Topics for Adults

Travel destinations

Health and well-being

Peace

Better relationships (e.g., with partner, children, or colleagues)

Family

Meditating

Friends

Your dreams

Money

Sports

Smiling more

Overcoming something

Change diet (eating habits), eat healthy food

Career: new job or promotion

Giving up bad habit or habits

Material things (e.g., car, electrical appliances, or furniture)

Home improvements or new home

Self-confidence

Home life

Balance

Marriage

Love

Time

Happiness

Solving a problem

Simplifying your life

Exercising

Money

Sleeping more

Deep breathing

Helping others

Being grateful for what I have

Trust

Positive Affirmations for Adults

You can cut out these statements and use them on your vision board.

Amazing opportunities are everywhere.
The world's my oyster.
I can do anything that I set my mind on.
I enjoy my own company.
I love being me.
I attract loving people.
My family supports me in all ways.
I love myself.
Today is going to be a great day.
Dreams can and do come true.
I accept myself just the way I am.
I am beautiful in every single way.
I am fit and healthy.
I now have a wonderful partner.
I trust that everything will work out just fine.
Life is really good to me.
I deserve the best.
I have great friends who support me.
I get enough sleep each night.
I make time for me, as I am important.
I love to travel and explore the world.
Any obstacle is there to teach me something positive.
I eat healthy foods because I care for my body.
I accept others as they are.
My job gives me much satisfaction.
I think positive words.
When I need peace, I take three deep breaths.
Money comes to me easily and effortlessly.
The sky's the limit.
My job gives me much pleasure.
Today is going to be a fabulous day.

I always have enough time in my day.
I cherish every moment.
I do what I love, and I do it often.
I am rich in all areas of life.
I see the good in every situation
My home life is wonderful.

Background Music for Making Adult Vision Boards

Following is a list of the songs that I recommend adults listen to while making a vision board. However, you can use any music you love.

"Walking on Sunshine," Katrina and the Waves

"What a Wonderful World," Louie Armstrong

"Walk of Life," Dire Straits

"Always Look on the Bright Side of Life," Monty Python

"I Want to Break Free," Queen

"Beautiful Day," U2

"I Gotta Feeling," Black Eyed Peas

"Just Dance," Lady Gaga

"Your Love Is Lifting Me Higher," Jackie Wilson

"Get the Party Started," Pink

"I'll Be There for You," The Rembrandts

"Count on Me," Bruno Mars

"You Raise Me Up" Josh Groban

"Footloose," Kenny Loggins

"Celebration," Kool and the Gang

"Old Time Rock and Roll," Bob Seger and the Silver Bullet Band

Examples of Adult Vision Boards

Louise made this vision board in a workshop I ran. She wanted to get tickets to see Rob Thomas, the lead singer from Matchbox Twenty, on his solo tour. She cut out a picture of him and put it on the vision board displayed here. That night, she got the tickets, no problem. Louise had the best night at the concert, and Rob Thomas even recognised her in the audience! this occurred because Louise and her friends all wore the same coloured t-shirt with the same saying on the front in the audience. She took a photo of herself on face book with the same t-shirt. She posted the photo online to Rob Thomas to let him know that she will be right at the front of his concert with her groupie friends all wearing the same t-shirt.

Tammy's Vision Board
Label: Gold Coast Family Fun
My husband found good deals online and suggested we go to
the Gold Coast for a family holiday, so off we're going.

Label: Create Space
We have demolished two small garden sheds and now have one large garage,
which will house all the things causing clutter. Yay! More space!

Vision Boards by Defence Mothers

A group of defence mothers worked on vision boards at the school to focus on many areas of their lives to improve and change. High on their list of importance was a good night's sleep and self-esteem. They found making their vision boards enjoyable, and as you can see, there were lots of laughs!

Michael decided to make the above vision board to improve his health and to focus on a long-awaited holiday as well as some material things that were hard to manifest. After making his board, his health improved, a holiday to Alice Springs happened, and material items came to him easily.

The adult that made this vision board achieved going on a holiday, making bathroom renovations, and publishing a book. I wonder who that was.

A teacher at the school where I work made this vision board at the start of 2013, and within a year she became engaged. She also brought a house with her partner at the end of 2013.

The following words can be used to cut out and paste on your vision board.

LOVE	Change
Dream	*Amazing*
I CAN DO IT.	**Brilliant**
Happiness	Great
I am ...	**I am ...**
Home	**Life**
TIME	Beauty
Travel	*Holiday*
I LOVE ...	**Believe**

Positive	Body
Lucky	**Job**
Money	**Magic**
CAN	Deserve
I now	*Lovely*
AWESOME	**Super**
Friends	Sport
Confidence	**Grateful**
Focus	**Calm**

RICH	Home
Trust	*Achieve*
EXERCISE	**Holiday**
I like …	Rest
Spoil	**Wish**
Work	**Success**
JOY	Future
Power	*Create*
ATTRACT	**I have …**

Laugh	True
Blessings	**Heal**
Breathe	**Thanks**
ALIVE	Universe
Hope	*Talented*
MEDITATE	**Joy**
Happy	Smart
Trust	**Good**
Make	**Faith**

You can add pictures to a cork board. When a goal has been achieved, you can unpin the picture and replace it with a new goal. This way, you only have one vision board at a time as mentioned previously.

Vision Boards for Children

Why Vision Boards Are Great for Children

Vision boards are an excellent tool for children. It starts them early with focusing on a goal and helping them strive for it.

The goal needs to be easy and achievable, and it is advised that the younger the child is, the better it is to focus on one goal at a time. Therefore, each year the child gets older (starting at age five), he or she can focus on more areas at a time.

In the classroom, vision boards can be used for various subjects in which the teacher would like children to show improvement. For example, they could be used for children that need help with spelling words, behaviour issues, staying on task, making new friends, and many more areas.

There are many methods for making a vision board in the classroom. Children can make a placemat that is then laminated and put on their desk. This allows them to see their goal all the time. It could also be laminated near where they sit or hung elsewhere in the classroom. Perhaps you could make a mobile to hang from the ceiling, and the child can put positive traits above themselves. For example, if a girl's name is Savannah, she could choose the attributes smart, funny, happy, friendly, kind, and so forth.

Children could make a poster and then write, "I am …" and add a picture.

31

Another way is to make a book holding positive words and pictures on each page. The children can read their own book each day for a week or two to be instilled with positivity.

Children could also cut out positive pictures and situations and then put them on paper as a collage. This works just as well.

The child can bring a picture of him or herself from home and affix it in the middle of a sheet of poster paper. Then the boy or girl can cut out positive words from this book and stick them around the photo.

I suggest including a few positive affirmations on a page. Children can either write these out themselves or find letters in magazines or newspapers and cut them out. They could even type affirmations on the computer and print them out. The child also needs to put his or her name with the affirmations.

Vision Board Topics for Children

A child can use this list to focus on one area at a time, as previously described.

Listening to my teacher in class
Listening at home
Staying on task
Having a happy face
Reading
Writing
Smiling
Eating a new vegetable or fruit
Doing my chores at home
I do ...
I am ...
I can ...
I love ...
I see ...
Trying hard
Friendships
Grieving for a loved one or pet
Improving in a sport
Keeping my room tidy
Saving money for a goal
Finding a hobby
Practicing good manners
Singing
Having fun

Positive Affirmations for Children

Listed below are some examples to use. Simply cut out the sentences and use them on your vision board, or you can write your own.

I listen …
I love my family.
I can read.
I am good.
I am kind.
I listen to my mum and dad.
I am happy.
I like …
I am lucky.
I can do anything.
I love …
I do my best.
I share …
I like my friends.
I love watching my favourite show.
I love to play.
I love having fun.
I laugh a lot.
I am safe.
I feel better now.
My family loves me.
I am funny.
I am really good at …
I love school.
I am smart.
I have nice friends.
I am spectacular.
I tried hard.
I love hugs.

I am awesome.

I love eating ...

I love my mum and dad.

I love my dog (or cat, fish, or other animal).

I love listening to ...

Background Music Making for Children's Vision Boards

"What Makes You Beautiful," One Direction	(ages 8 to adult)
"The Hamster Dance," Hampton the Hampster	(ages 2 to 10)
"Hot Potato," The Wiggles	(ages 1 to 6)
"Chicken Dance," The Emeralds	(ages 3 to adult)
"You've Got a Friend in Me," Randy Newman	(ages 1 to adult)
"Roar," Katy Perry	(ages 7 to adult)
"Royals," Lorde	(ages 10 to adult)
"What Does the Fox Say?" Ylvis	(ages 12 to adult)
"Macarena," Los Del Rio	(ages 8 to adult)
"Happy," Pharrell Williams	(ages 1 to adult)
"Gangnam Style," Psy	(ages 10 to adult)
"Who Let the Dogs Out," Baha Men	(ages 1 to adult)
"YMCA," Village People	(ages 7 to adult)
"Don't Worry, Be Happy," Bobby McFerrin	(ages 5 to adult)

Pictures of Children's Vision Boards

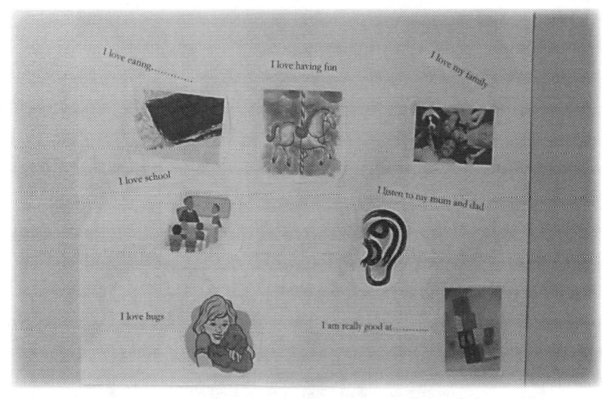

This vision board was made by cutting out affirmations from this book and using clip art.

A ten-year-old used the positive words from
this book to make this vision board.

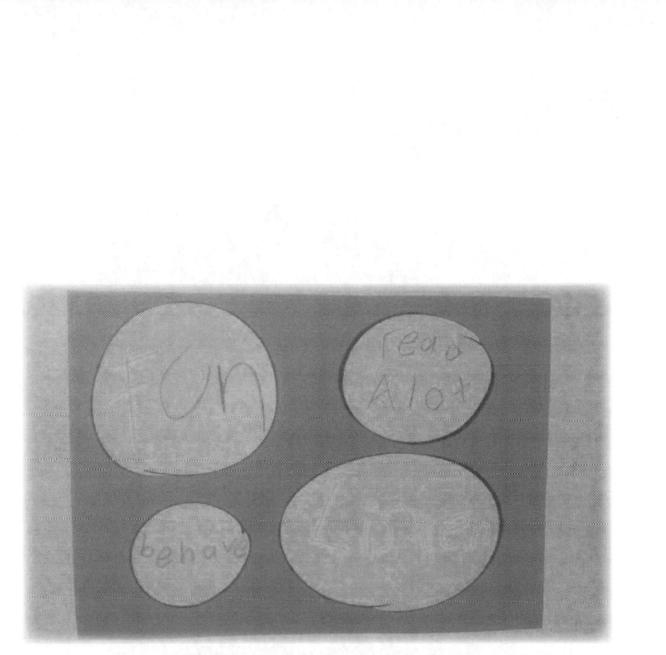

This child wrote their words in bubbles, and the focus was school.

The above vision board was made on the computer,
using fonts, word art, and a border.

The following words can be used to cut out and paste on your vision board.

FUN	Sing
Laugh	*School*
I CAN DO IT	**Friends**
Happy	Great
I love	**I am**
Home	**Friends**
I LIKE	Family
My pet	*I try*
DO MY BEST	**Listen**

41

Funny	Sport
I am	**I am**
Play	**I can**
READ	Write
Draw	*Spell*
GOOD	**Love**
Games	Party
Paint	**Food**
Kids	**Toys**

SMILE	Make
Holiday	*TV show*
COLOUR IN	**Sleep**
Cartoons	Great
Space	**Dream**
Award	**Music**

Vision Boards for Teenagers

Why Vision Boards are Great for Teenagers

Having a vision board helps you focus on your goals and dreams.

It is a great tool when you need to build your self-confidence. By putting positive words on your board, the intention attracts the ability to change your circumstances. In fact, the energy around words helps bring the personality traits that you want.

You need something to look forward to, and a vision board allows you to use your imagination about what you would like to achieve.

You can do a vision board for any area of your life, from anything at home, at school, or a sporting achievement, to self-worth or behaviour issues that you would like to change.

It is fun and very easy to do. All you need is an hour.

Why don't you give it a go? Once you have done one, you will feel good, and it may bring you positive change.

The next few pages list topics that you can use, or you might think of another topic. There are also affirmations in the following pages that you may want to use, or you can come up with your own.

47

Vision Board Topics for Teenagers

Being happy

Getting great grades

Being on time

Being more organised in class or my room

Appreciating wonderful teachers

Eating healthy foods

Drinking more water

Wonderful relationships with family or friends

Staying on task

Having confidence

Being positive

Improving in sport

Caring for my pets

Overcoming something

Getting rid of a bad habit (e.g., biting my nails)

Making good choices

Asking for help

Something I love doing

Having more love in my life

Being grateful for ...

Getting along with others

Having a happy home

Exercising

Communicating

Developing hobbies

Experiencing love

Positive Affirmations for Teenagers

These can be cut out and used on vision boards.

I am smart.

I am friendly.

I am confident.

I am always on time for school.

I am happy.

I am a good listener.

I always do my best at school.

I always see the positive in every situation.

I have a lot of patience.

I am a wonderful person.

I have a lot of great qualities.

I am grateful for what I have in my life.

I have a great personality.

I make friends easily.

I love my family.

I am intelligent.

I am funny.

I focus on one task at a time.

I make good decisions.

I love being me.

I love everything about myself.

I can do anything.

I make time for homework.

I take care of my body by eating healthy foods.

I am good at ...

I love ...

I love doing ...

I am ...

I ask for help when I need it.

I love playing a sport (e.g., soccer, tennis, etc.).

I love listening to music.

I am calm.

I am helpful.

I have a lot to offer.

I am important.

I matter.

I am a fabulous person.

I am unique.

I love spending time with …

I speak with confidence.

I value myself.

I am a lovely person.

I am special.

I take three deep breaths to calm down.

I make a difference.

I love myself.

I always do my best.

My ideal job is …

I enjoy my own company.

I get at least eight hours sleep per night.

My passion is …

I look forward to each day.

I love my family.

Background Music for Making Teenagers' Vision Boards

"Absolutely Everybody," Vanessa Amorosi

"You're My Best Friend," Queen

"Shiny Happy People," R.E.M.

"Best Night," Justice Crew

"Party Rock Anthem," LMFAO

"Smash Mouth," All Star

"Call Me Maybe," Carly Rae Jepsen

"Count on Me," Bruno Mars

"Paradise," Coldplay

"Story of My Life," One Direction

"Things Can Only Get Better," D:Rream

Pictures of Teenage Vision Boards

You can put your name in the middle of your poster and
write or paste positive words all around it.

This poster has the year in the middle, surrounded by
all the goals this teenager wants to achieve.

My Family

This vision board was made using photographs and
decorative text from a computer program.

LOVE	Change
Dream	*Amazing*
I CAN DO IT.	**Brilliant**
Happiness	Great
I am	**I am**
Home	**Life**
BODY	Unique
Listen	*Dream*
MUSIC	**Future**

Relax	Money
Play	**Work**
Life	**Family**
DRIVE	Sport
Passion	*Inspire*
WIN	**Race**
Exercise	Movie
Travel	**Test**
Study	**Friends**

TIME	Ask
Sleep	*Healthy*
CONFIDENCE	**Time**
Wish	Save
Free	**Calm**
Hobby	**Nature**

Phrases to Use or Not Use on Your Vision Board

The phrases "I am" and "I have" are life changing. When you use them on a vision board, you're making that statement to the universe. For example, writing, "I am confident," helps create confidence in you. Another example could be writing. "I love my life." This, in turn, allows you to start loving life more. These powerful statements allow situations to take place in the near future. Using the phrase "I am" allows your mind to believe that this statement is true, which makes changes occur. The phrases "I can" and "I know" in addition to the previously mentioned ones are powerful when you use them on your vision board. You can also use these words while expressing yourself in speeches or written essays.

Here are some more examples of powerful statements:

I am smart.
I am successful.
I can do anything.
I have the potential to achieve anything.
I now have more time to do the things that I love.
Some phrases are better not to use on a vision board: I wish, I don't, I can't, and I won't. They stop you from achieving your goals and produce negative situations. Words have powerful energy when they are spoken, thought, felt.

I wish I had a car.
I don't want that to happen.

61

I can't—it's too hard.
I won't be able to achieve that.

The above sentences have a lower vibrational energy when said or written compared with the preceding positive ones.. Can you feel negative energy connecting to you when you make these statements?

Two Examples of "I am" or "I love" Vision Boards

Jake wanted to focus on being on task at school,
so he put this on his vision board.

This vision board may make more love come into someone's life in the different areas that the person mentioned.

Attracting What You Want: Six-Month, One-Year, and Five-Year Plan

In my mid-twenties, I wanted to attract the right type of man, as in the past I only attracted unsuitable partners. So I decided to do a six-month, one-year and five-year plan. I wrote half a page of qualities that I wanted in my life partner for the six-month plan. I met my partner, now my husband, in just less than six months. I had written a one-year plan two years into our relationship, that I would like to have a house and be married, and that happened six months later. The five-year plan was to have two children, and that happened within the first year of the five-year plan. In my long-term plan, I also put down that I'd like a job not too far from home that I could walk to if I needed to and that I would be making a difference. At the end of the five years, I got the job at the school, and it filled all of those requirements. These are just some of the amazing things that happen when you write down and visualize what you want. I have helped a lot of friends who were single for many years with this technique, and it works.

To get started, all you need is a piece of paper and pen or a computer or tablet to write or type.

Think carefully about what you want—for example, perhaps a lovely relationship, better health, a job, and so forth.

Focus on whether you will focus on a six-month, one-year, or five-year plan. You can start with the three pages I've included in this section.

65

On your paper or the computer, write this sentence after labelling the time period: "I [your name], on this day [the month, day, and year], ask the universe to bring to me …" Describe in detail the thing or person, such as wanting a lovely man that has similar qualities to come into your life. You might specify that he is loving, kind, helpful, understands you, has a job, is sensitive, and the like. Put down positive qualities important to you. This technique will help you manifest what it is that you want. As mentioned previously, you don't get your full desire if you're undecided. You can do a page or two if you like. There are so many areas that you can cover, from a holiday, to having more confidence or attracting the right type of friends; the choices are endless. If, for example, you want to attract a house or an overseas holiday, I would make the plan for one year or five years, as some things take a bit longer to manifest.

Once you are done, read your plan to make sure that you're happy with it. Then you can fold up your handwritten letter, print a copy, or save it on your computer. Read it through once more, and then put it away and don't focus on it anymore. By doing this, you're letting it go and allowing the law of attraction to bring your goal to you. Once a month, read it to yourself at a time when you are in a positive frame of mind. This process is powerful, and it will help bring you what you want. It has helped me in so many areas, and I have passed this on to many people over the years with much success.

You can photocopy the following pages and use them over and over.

Six-Month Plan

One-Year Plan

Five-Year Plan

Programming Your Day

Programming your day means visualizing and creating your day before it happens. When you wake up in the morning, half asleep in bed, focus on what you want to happen. If, for example, you are meeting up with a friend or loved one at a park, visualize the surroundings at the park and picture both of you there. Now visualize the two of you talking nicely and having a great time. This programs the situation, and you can create the best possible outcome. You can use this method for all sorts of scenarios, such as going to a job interview, attending a wedding, entering an awkward situation, or going on a holiday; you can also do it when you want a close spot in a car park at your favourite shopping centre at Christmas time.

First thing in the morning is the best time to do this, as people are usually more open to insights at this time. When we are not fully awake yet, our state of mind brings information to help and inspire us. I call it our higher self, and it gives us help and positive advice. When I get up, the first thing I do is have a shower, and a lot of great ideas and advice come up.

I highly recommend this method. You are the creator of your life, so why not create your day the way you like? Spend at least five minutes focusing on what you want with good feelings. And then just let it go and trust that all will turn out well.

Making a Vision Board Using Your Computer

You can also make a vision board by using your computer, laptop, or mobile device. I have done this using a mobile app called Dreamboard Mobile. It includes templates, affirmations, and backgrounds that can be added. Some templates are free. You can update this app at any time and save what you have done. The basic features are free, but some require an extra fee. Please note this app may not be available in all countries.

When you use your computer, you can cut and paste as many times as you like. Oprah's website, www.oprah.com, has a vision board program. You will need to sign up to access it. I had success using it, as my vision to write a book on vision boards to help others came true.

You can use any font that you like in any size. Make your own affirmations, and add as many as you can fit.

You can download photos that you have taken and add them to your vision board, add affirmations, and use clip art. You can really go far when using the computer. If you're not completely happy with something on the screen, you can delete it at any time. Once finished, you can save your masterpiece or print it.

You can use any font that you like in any size. Make your own affirmations, and add as many as you can fit.

About the Author

Tania Chumbley is a school services officer from Adelaide, South Australia. It became apparent to her in 2008 that making vision boards manifested situations and material items quite easily. Tania has implemented vision boards at the school where she works and also with adults in positive development classes she runs. She has received a lot of positive feedback and heard wonderful stories of how vision boards have helped people's dreams come true.

She now wants to share her easy techniques in this workbook, which includes step-by-step instructions on how to make vision boards for all ages.

About the Book

Making a vision board is a fun activity to do by yourself, with friends, or in the classroom.

It is a great tool for teachers to use with their students. Parents can help their children and teenagers make vision boards about certain areas of their life the young people want to improve. A vision board is also great for those of us adults who are ready for changes and making decisions about what we want in life.

This book is for adults, teenagers, and children, and it includes all the instructions you'll need to make your own vision boards. It contains inspiring words ready for you to cut out and paste on your board and positive affirmations.

Let this book help make your dreams become a reality.

Tania also included the following:

Supplies you need to make a vision board

Subjects to focus on

Pictures of actual vision boards to get ideas

How to set goals and program your day

Ideas for background music to inspire you while making your vision board

And much more